Written by
Nicola
Chave

Like Yours, Like Mine

FACES

KidHaven
PUBLISHING

Published in 2027 by
KidHaven Publishing, an Imprint of Greenhaven Publishing, LLC
2544 Clinton St., Buffalo, NY 14224

Written by: Nicola Chave
Edited by: Beth Latham
Designed by: Ian McMullen

Cataloging-in-Publication Data

Names: Chave, Nicola.
Title: Faces / Nicola Chave.
Description: Buffalo, NY : KidHaven Publishing, 2027. | Series: Like yours, like mine | Includes glossary and index.
Identifiers: ISBN 9781534570887 (pbk.) | ISBN 9781534570894 (library bound) | ISBN 9781534570900 (ebook)
Subjects: LCSH: Face--Juvenile literature. | Human body--Juvenile literature.
Classification: LCC QM535.C438 2027 | DDC 611.92 --dc23

Printed in the United States

CPSIA compliance information: Batch #CS27KH: For further information contact Greenhaven Publishing LLC at 1-844-317-7404.

Please visit our website, www.greenhavenpublishing.com.
For a free color catalog of all our high-quality books, call toll free 1-844-317-7404 or fax 1-844-317-7405.

Find us on

IMAGE CREDITS
Images courtesy of Shutterstock.com, unless otherwise stated.
Cover - PeopleImages, Quality Stock Arts, Monkey Business Images.
4-5 - Rawpixel.com, Denis Kuvaev. 6-7 - Pixel-Shot, Ukraine_riakhin, New Africa, Cat Simpson, Master1305, Kittyfly. 8-9 - Rido, Pixel-Shot, DmyTo, New Africa. 10-11 - StoryTime Studio, MY STOCKERS, Oleg Golovnev, Best smile studio, Peakstock. 12-13 - Sorapop Udomsri, ViDI Studio, soumen82hazra, anatoliy_gleb. 14-15 - Viktoriia Hnatiuk, soumen82hazra, SeventyFour, K-Shoot Background, Chiarascura. 16-17 - Odua Images, chomplearn, Studio Romantic. 18-19 - Pat Sprada, Odua Images, LightField Studios, andreonegin, Prostock-studio. 20-21 - Simol1407, Vershinin89, LightField Studios, India Picture. 22-23 - Rawpixel.com, Rido.

CONTENTS

Words that look like THIS can be found in the glossary on page 24.

EVERYONE IS UNIQUE

Our world is an amazing place. It is a planet full of billions of people. Every person is different and **UNIQUE**. No two people are the same!

Let's explore the wonderful world of human faces!

So many things help make us who we are. When you think of someone, you might picture their face. Your face is part of what makes you YOU!

EYES

The middle of the human eye is called the pupil. The colored part of the eye is called the iris. Human eyes come in six main **NATURAL** colors. These are...

Even if they look like they are the same color, no two people's eyes are the same.

Some people have a pupil that isn't round. This is called a coloboma.

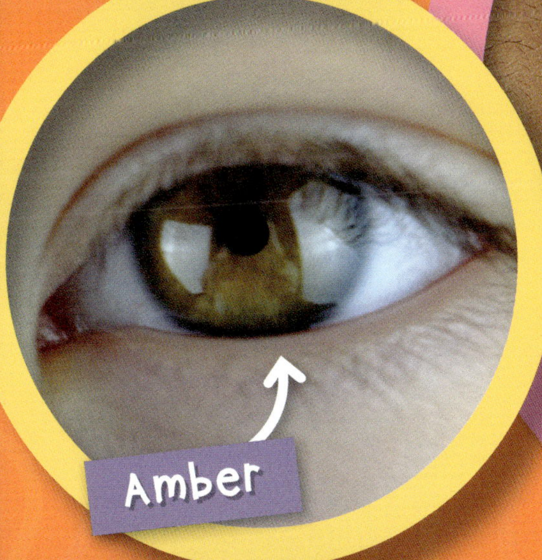

Some people wear glasses over their eyes to help them see clearly. Nearsightedness is when people cannot see faraway objects clearly. Farsightedness is when people find it difficult to clearly see things that are close to them.

Some people might wear **CONTACT LENSES** instead of glasses.

Some people might not have an eye. They might wear a **PROSTHETIC** eye in its place. Prosthetic eyes cannot help a person see, but they can make people feel more confident.

Prosthetic eyes can be molded and painted to make them unique.

EARS

Ears are very important because they help people hear the world around them. Ears can be different shapes and sizes. Some might be bigger, and some might be smaller. Some can be hairy.

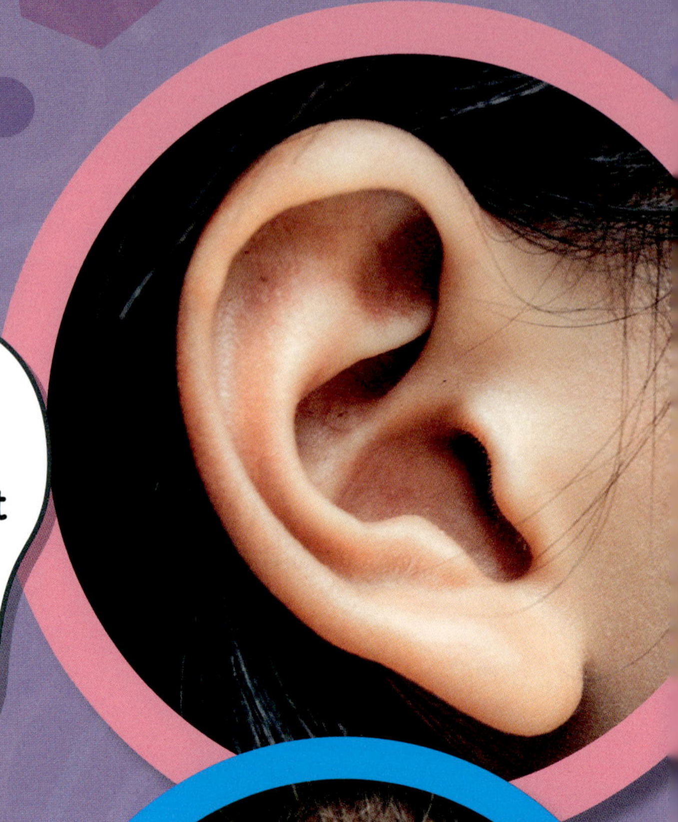

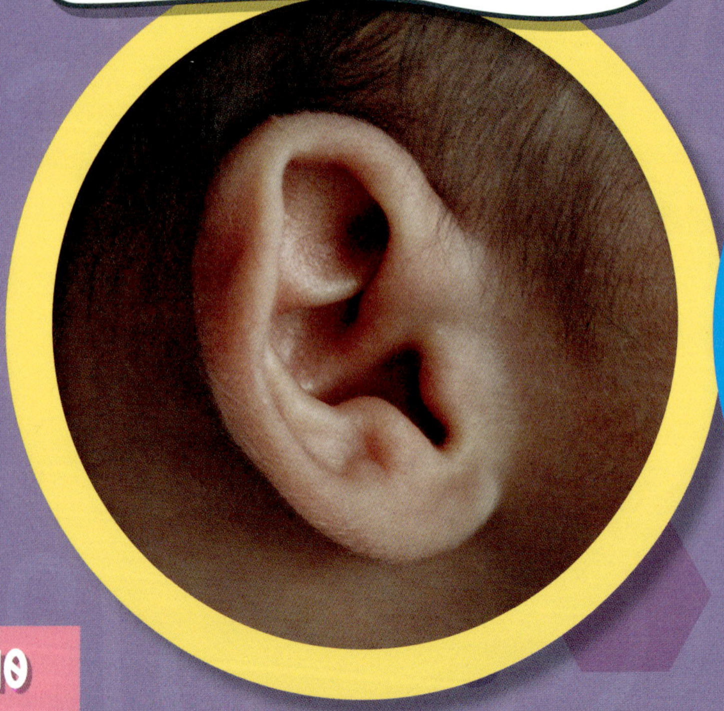

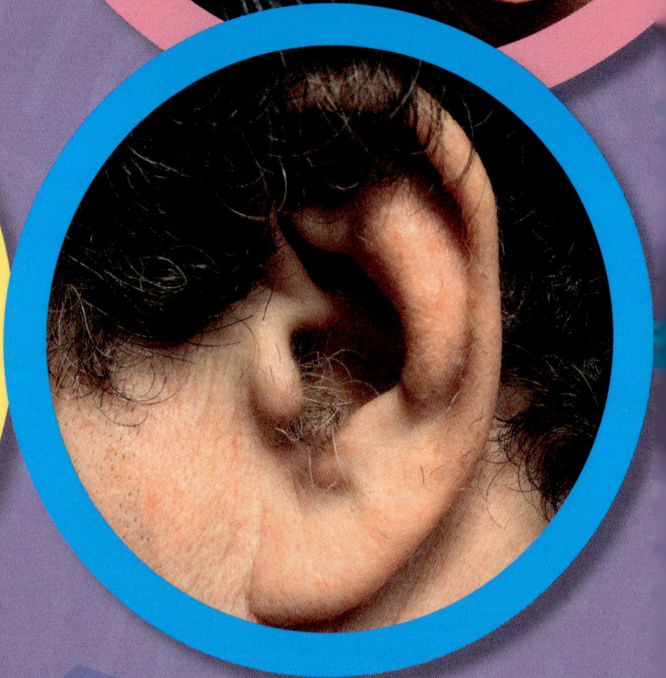

Some people find it difficult to hear or might not be able to hear at all. This is called being hard of hearing or deaf. Hearing aids and cochlear implants can help people hear things.

TEETH

When you open your mouth or smile, you can see your teeth. When children grow, they lose their baby teeth. This is very normal. It is to make room for adult teeth. Most adults have 32 teeth.

The last teeth to grow are called wisdom teeth. Some people never grow wisdom teeth.

Sometimes when adult teeth come in, they might be crooked. Some people get braces to make their teeth straighter. Braces are very common. They can come in lots of different colors.

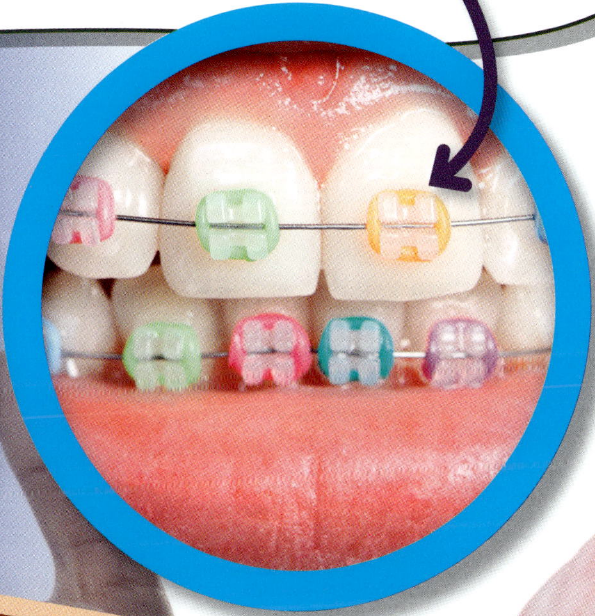

Always brush your teeth to keep them healthy and strong!

SKIN

The skin on a person's face is rarely all one color or **TEXTURE**. Skin can be covered in freckles, moles, pimples, scars, or birthmarks.

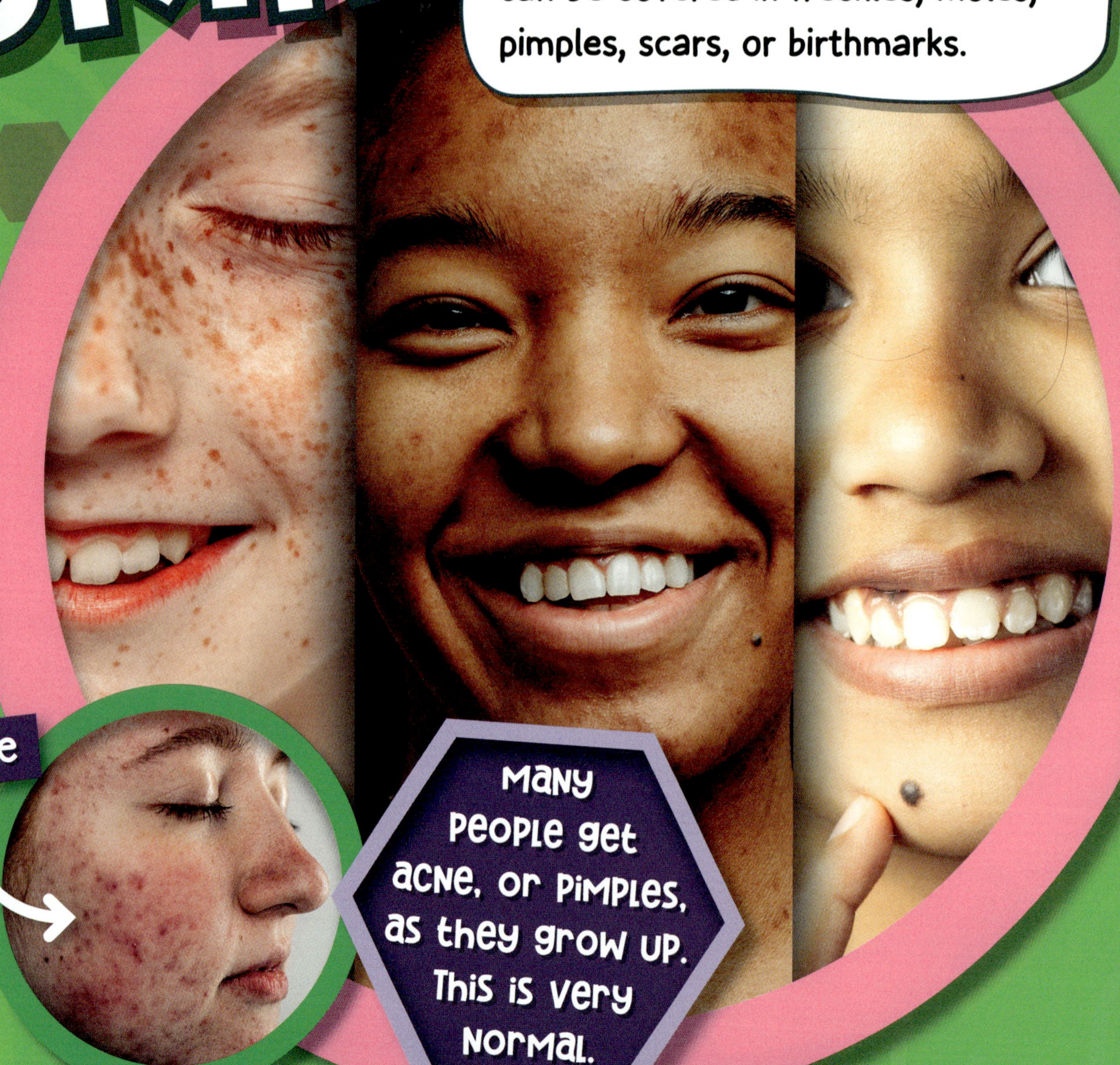

Many people get acne, or pimples, as they grow up. This is very normal.

Wrinkles, such as laugh lines, might appear on a person's face as they grow older. Wrinkles are a normal sign of growing older. They show all the times we've smiled, laughed, and frowned.

FACIAL COVERINGS

Some people choose to cover their faces for religious or **CULTURAL** reasons. Some Muslim women and girls might choose to wear a niqab or a burka. These are pieces of fabric that cover a person's face.

Sometimes, people might wear surgical masks for health reasons. Some people need to wear these masks as part of their job. When you visit the dentist, you might see lots of people wearing these masks.

MAKEUP

Makeup is a beautiful and fun way to be creative and express your personality. There are lots of different types of makeup. Some makeup is bold and colorful, and other types are more **SUBTLE**.

Anyone can wear makeup, and there is no right or wrong way to wear it. Some people wear a lot of makeup to express themselves. Other people might wear just a little bit. Some people choose not to wear any makeup.

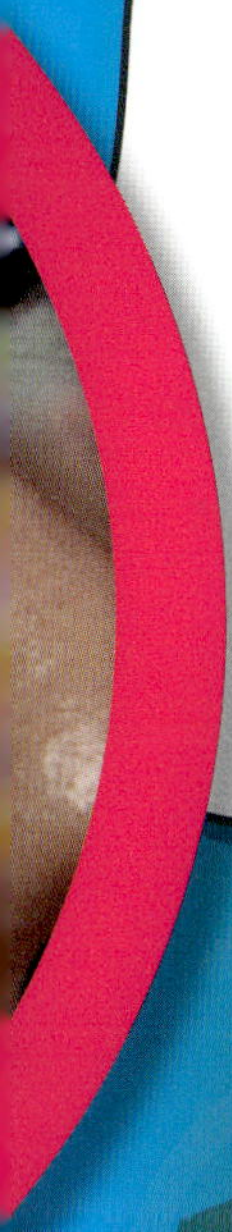

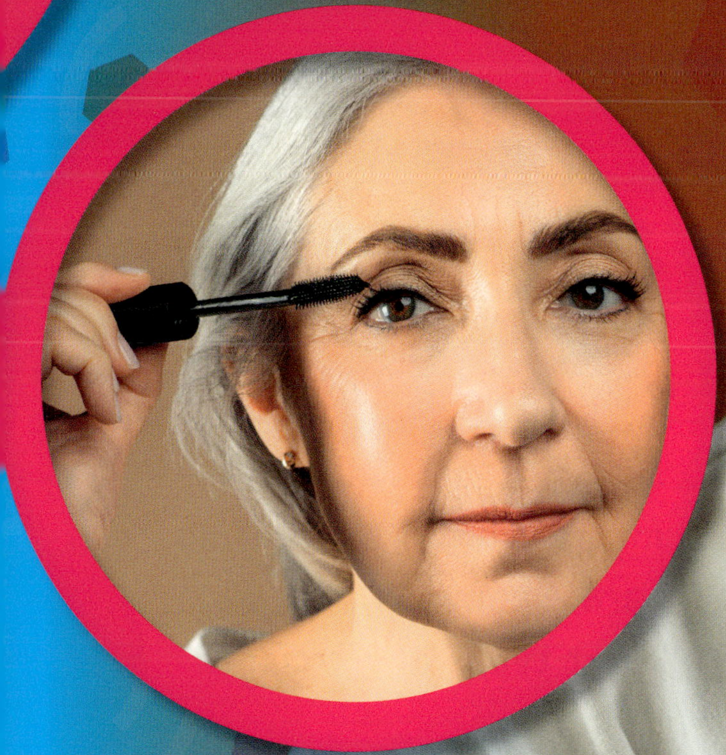

PIERCINGS

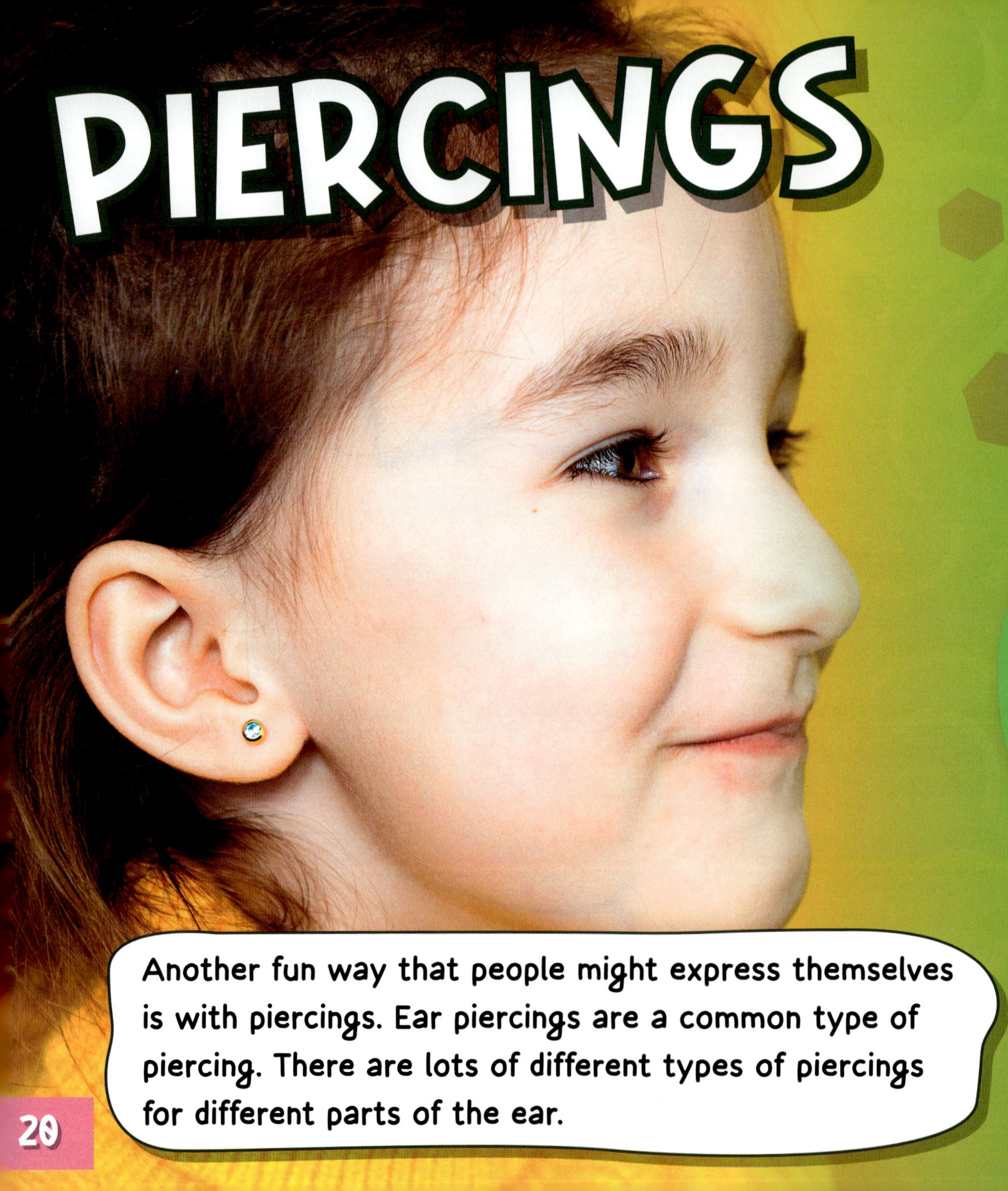

Another fun way that people might express themselves is with piercings. Ear piercings are a common type of piercing. There are lots of different types of piercings for different parts of the ear.

Sometimes, people might get other parts of their face pierced. There are nose studs, nose rings, eyebrow piercings, tongue piercings, and lip piercings. Many of these can only be done when the person is an adult.

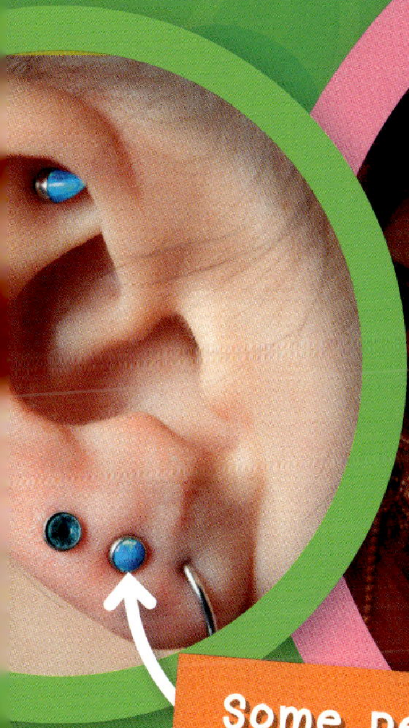

Some people get one ear piercing, but other people get lots.

Piercings should always be done safely and by a **PROFESSIONAL**.

WHAT ABOUT YOUR FACE?

All faces are amazing, and everyone's face is different. No two people look exactly the same. Even identical twins have small differences. Our faces help make us **DIVERSE** and unique.

Does your face have pimples or freckles? Have you lost any teeth, or do you wear braces? Does your nose crinkle when you smile? What makes your face special? Remember, your face is beautiful, and so are you!

GLOSSARY

contact lenses
small, thin discs worn on the eye to improve sight

cultural
to do with the traditions, ideas, and ways of life of a particular group of people

diverse
a way of describing a group of varied and different things

natural
found in nature and not made by people

professional
someone who has trained to do a particular job

prosthetic
a human-made body part

subtle
difficult to spot

texture
the feel of something

unique
unlike anything or anyone else

INDEX